# distant transit

## poems by Maja Haderlap

translated from the German by Tess Lewis

Library of Congress Cataloging-in-Publication Data available upon request

Archipelago Books
232 3rd Street #A111
Brooklyn, NY 11215
www.archipelagobooks.org

Distributed by Penguin Random House
www.penguinrandomhouse.com

Cover art: Joseph Beuys
Book design: Zoe Guttenplan

This work is made possible by the New York State Council on the Arts with the support of
the Office of the Governor and the New York State Legislature. Funding for the
translation of this book was provided by a grant from the Carl Lesnor Family Foundation.

This publication was made possible with support from Lannan Foundation,
the National Endowment for the Arts, the New York City Department of Cultural Affairs,
and the Austrian Federal Ministry for Art, Culture, Public Service and Sport.

   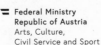 

PRINTED IN THE UNITED STATES

*contents*

### house of love

# distant transit

almost homeward

## piran

in the house next door there's a coming and going,
but the spindle tree shields me from sight.
the overgrown garden is crossed only
by paths for cats, toads and snails.
noisily, the sea shakes off its stenchcoat.
on my desk, fictional characters
practice missing dialogue.
i sit here as if at the root of an old disturbance,
forcing air into my memory cells
to keep them alive, in the evening
i cross the piazza tartini and return
in the morning with fresh melons from the market.
twice a week, frida comes by.
why don't you marry, she calls from the bushes,
it's still better than being alone.
today a toad will lose its warts
when i kiss it, i say.
then i'd like to be your maid of honor, my dear poet.
again a door clicks shuts.

**trieste trst triest**

did the seagulls detect your vanishing point,
city of paper, city entranced by words,
shouted at from all directions
when it came time to rally around another name.
city that retreats behind a defensive wall
of palazzi. your manor houses always looked like barracks,
military cemeteries and war memorials led
through the villages to you. the border tightened
your steel collar. when your liberators stormed
in, sunken goods were unloaded in the port
like things extinguished. the sea beats roughly against
the jetty, the bora lashes your stiff timberwork.
poets cast in bronze bustle through your backstreets
without a word, because they saw you
when you still believed yourself to be more than
your nation's façade. in your bay
my language encountered the glistening sea,
fell out of its crib onto the shore, was
still at home, was no longer alone.
here i practiced kissing with a view
of the adriatic, my freezing hands
buried in a man's coat. tongue between
teeth and elsewhere. the gulls in the updraft.

## komen

our day began late.
it had slept through the morning,
trotted behind us. we remained
seated on a stone bench, where all
couples turn to stone. a campanile
called back those birds that had
fled. a wall of yews intruded
into the picture and the ornamental pond rose
to our throats. you explained all the fishes
that circled around us. that one is slinging
its hook, you said, it won't live
much longer. a plane hovered
endlessly over the small cloud.
the hedge bore fruit again.
a white poodle ran toward us.
it takes itself too seriously, you said.
for years a nightingale has perched on
this verse and we two in front of it,
on our day.

## karst meadow near col

when the shepherds' whistles cut through
the air, so shrill they sounded
as if they were coming from the century before last,
still rushing away from the cracking whip,
the grass grew rampant over the meadow.
the dry stone walls held slipping layers tight,
spread their shielding stones over
the bumblebees, wasps and lizards,
the gnarled oak trees, the unwieldy
barberry wrenched at the stone strip.
(the wild sage just moved closer
to the juniper bush guardian.)
a vortex formed in the meadow and everything
was swallowed up in its thundering eye, the calls
of the shepherds, the farmers' names,
the sheep barrows and goat stalls,
the enclosed islands of warmth
in which the bora lay down, with a docile
flicker. all of a sudden the moment rose
up, thrust me into the grass torrent,
threw itself in my path.

## lagoon near grado

don't know if i was the one
who went with you into the lagoon. was
it my mother, my sister,
another relative you took in
your arms, although
when i embraced you
you were your father, your son, your wife.
behind my back the mountains
looked like they had been piled up from foam.
they seeped sluggishly into the sea. here
the islands ran aground on silt,
the current exposed old routes
and immediately erased them. the brackish
light smelled of pools and seaweed.
we went towards the levee and overtook
the waves that had rushed out ahead of us
towards the mosaics of aquileia.
i looked at you with disparate eyes,
i am and am not that.
intermediate land, unseparated.

## hay sheds in laze

i stepped abruptly into time's rear courtyard,
into the chink of time that stared impassively.
under the ash-copse before me stood
the sheds, stricken with the lichen of age,
derelict. as if year after year the ricks had been shaken by
the seconds' tremors, they caved in,
no longer thought much of themselves. as lepers
they were once banished behind the crest
of the hill, where there was nothing to till,
no garden, no field, where neither human
nor animal shelters stood in anyone's way or cornered
their dwellers in constriction,
in bias. under the corrugated metal roof
the smallest of doors, through which only the lankest
creature and a pitiful man could
slip. here destiny ordained who was to leave,
who would hurriedly abandon his barrels, scythes
and wheels, the crudely timbered
granaries, the chestnut basket, the straw door,
the last wisps of straw in decrepit wooden huts. those who
could not give up dreaming stood on
the deck of an ocean liner and waved
at those who stayed home. carrying in their luggage

the story of *lepa vida* like blind passengers.
underneath, wrapped in an old shirt,
the memory of Mount Matajur's crest
at dawn, when they set off.

**venezia**

we sit on the pier of this fish-city,
which swings on the hook of the tide
and cannot escape it. we talk about ourselves
and what holds us captive here
on the shore between north and south.
the mosaics of aquileia, I say,
the swaying dolphins and spiny lobsters,
that found refuge in trees from the great flood.
the snow-crowned alps that surge skywards
like an ossified, wildly agitated sea.
the timavo's dark maw, you say,
out of which the river surges as if it were
flowing from one abyss into the next,
the houses in this city, like mussels
washed ashore, weather-beaten and rotting.
the algae spreads like a carpet
at our feet. lines of words swim like lures
in the lagoons. we wait for the catch and laugh.
bubbles rise from our noses,
scales of stone fall from our eyes—
we are finally caught in this place's net.

## borderlands

their borderlines knotted a string
of snares and transgressions.
in the annals of division the boundary was inscribed
as victor. in wartime, the border strip
swung back and forth, villages
went astray, slid to
the periphery. their inhabitants
sealed their throats with crude locks,
stood watch over the silent crime scene
that i enter light-heartedly. often, followed by
their eyes, i took the armored path to a
neighboring land, to hear of earlier days,
when fences still lined the pastures
and a kindred echo bound
all the names. where a road once ran
its trace disappears. all is margin
and forgetting and transition.

## a summer day on the jaunfeld

what infuses the focal length of time?
a day, attenuated to a breath in
and out, a sky, beneath which we walk in place
no matter how far away we move?
clouds perhaps, that, lost in thought,
pull strings, the sound of a mouth harp
like a fluttering sketch entangled in the air.
it swings on its own over the crags,
the mica paths and shale ridges.
a strange man, or what might be
rushing ahead or following him? my leaping
lines, brandishing stories wildly
so that they'll be heard. red and black
or green resound, as if blurred.
no longer graspable, the image of the day on
the mountain ridge under the pines. time
that assimilates and seals itself off.

## košuta

from the cliff face silence
breaks off like a boulder and falls on me,
expires. the peak's cloud sister
sits enthroned above the flank
of košuta mountain, impassive, cold
and white. an imperious pain
gropes for my form, which
trembles from its embrace.
a lover who gets the better of
all the limbs he probes,
seeks out. he knows all about me,
whereas i forget myself.
where else am i, other than in my gaze
at the hairline crack in the stone? in
the feverish head that casts sparks
into the blue of this sky,
which seizes me, just as
the insistent pain has
already enflamed me. I glow here
until the mountain's shadow fades.

**goče return**

a village searches for the way back from
absence. backs to the wind,
houses cling to each other, the aged
heart of the village drifts
in all directions, walls
spotted as if from fever, as if smeared
with a charcoal pencil. the windows little more
than yawning crypts of desolation.
the crown of an elder tree affixed
to the leaky roof. torrents of light from the nearby
sea thunder over the brittle rock,
press the village against the sheltering
mountainside. here it stood, before it was left behind
in the updraft of progress with the ghosts
that follow it everywhere. here it will later
be gone, the highest mountain grows
in the hollow, sheer ice peers out from the grottoes over
the valley. in earlier days, carved into blocks,
it was carried to the ships, to trieste, all the way to africa.
far away from the night caravans carrying
the solidified water. the cargo clouded in
wintry breath that mirrored the moon.
and again a gust of light shakes

the covenanted walls, pushes the
village further inland, toward the irises
and the cinquefoil. almost homeward.

carantania

**i**

*We began with myths and later included actual events*
Michael Ondaatje, *Handwriting*

it began with the drift out of the ovum
of the world of ravenna, when they believed themselves
near the golfus occidentalis and west
of thrace. syria hovered over
their rapturous heads, continents
floated past like opalescent fish.
then the first slavic king appeared,
samo, as lonely prince, a frankish
merchant. who is this who's come here,
the peasants asked. i am the voice
of my neighbor, the new king said
and married twelve conquered women.
inclined to stone he was, this man whose
tribe settled close to the mountains. Year
after year he trod his land in reverse, saw cities turn
into hills and villages into fields that
preserved their shadows. from the iron mines
in his realm climbed bondsmen
accustomed to the skyless earth, to meager
light. they marveled, there was movement after all.

*And in our Book Of Victories*
*whenever you saw a parasol on the battlefield*
*you could identify the king within its shadow.*
Michael Ondaatje, *Handwriting*

no matter where we sent our kings,
they always returned as converted lords
remained elusive, unseen. domitian
recovered his son from the lakebed,
which he had ordered drained, then disappeared.
he was a miracle worker they said, he could move
mountains and control lightning above
the clouds, far more than gorazd, boruth
and hotimir dared. the first crossed
the border near thörl disguised as venus
and was exposed as a singer. the second rolled
out of a wine barrel in wittenberg and made
a career as a bible salesman. the third went into
the forest, saw oaks and fir trees grow into cedar
and palm, and believed
he was listening to the bird of paradise. before he found
his way back as a monk, a thousand years had passed.

## iii

tired of kings but undaunted,
the slovenes took matjaž corvinus
prisoner and imprisoned him in a
mountain, until better times, a last resort.
kingless, king-free, they gained land,
strengthened their borders by
pacing them off with words, with names,
they planted thresholds and sowed
fields, set paths, appropriated
tracks. cultivated a festering
word crop, no flower designed,
nor animal ever invented. while others
waged wars, their language
rolled out spits of land, marked the field margins
with axioms, solicited protection with
curses. every tree grew into
a guardian, even the ancestors returned as
jackdaws to the abandoned fields.
moreover, the word carried so much weight
that they long kept it to themselves, the
two-faced treasure, with measures
for large and small, right and wrong.

iv

when the germinating language had fully budded,
embayed, serrated, winged, feathered,
and its grammar seemed etched into alphabet,
when, through stories recounted, enemies were banished to sea,
to the forest, to the cities and people
spoke of unity, realized they were a gem
in the ground plan of Europe, a branch on the bough
of their languages, their rival came as neighbor and seemed
more familiar in his dealings, friendlier
than their giants, the ajdi, who had always raged
on the mountain tops. he came to evaluate, to
count them, but found their number hardly worth
much. decreased in number, without protective power,
its speakers immediately hurled spear-sentences at
the majority. lanceolate, fired into the airy land,
scorched. lined up, bridled, the small nation's
cavalry stood, in the full
dress of their embattled, forbidden language,
armed for a fractious battle.
only their misgivings kept their word.

**distant transit**

**house of old languages**

distraught bees buzz in the corridors
of my abandoned language.
birds of passage purge themselves in
rooms assailed and reviled
as if they were finally home – that is, there where
they once were. language
kept me in thrall to the world but left me
unsatisfied. were i to bite through it,
i would taste its desolation. i left little behind,
even if it was all that remained from the years
i'd combed through. momentous promises
piled up behind its porous, atrophied
walls, along with that sweet melody, that still sang
to me of milk and honey, although
the destruction was long evident. i finally
set out, followed by all i'd left behind.
it has reached its destination,
while i circle without end.

# home

in this place language also comes to me
as a confidante who knows every secret.
where i hid my first toy and
my mother's ring, where I buried
the stolen coins, made my first child
in the hay, rubbing my naked body against
a thigh and kissing a girl,
because babies came from kissing. where
the magnificent plastic gondola stood
that signaled to me in my sleep, where
to find the honeycomb or the candies
the baker sold. language opens
rotted doors, thrusts the dusty boards
from their brackets, reveals the buried stone.
it flies at my face like a flock of startled
swallows, confronts me as the smell of mold,
drops from the jagged armor and
hulls of kids' stuff like silt shed from all that was.
as soon as its bird heart beats calmly,
it shows its skin, appears unscathed and
hardly used. keep me safe, language,
wall me off against time.

## dreaming language

my small tongue dreams up
a land where it builds nests of words
to swarm out over the borders
that are not its own. it wants
to outgrow itself, to glide through distant
spirit paths of water or gas,
to dive down to deep sea vents,
to have a term for every phenomenon
and its dubious shadows, to inhabit
those who speak and write it
as shimmering populations of words, to lay
its larvae in their pores. my language
wants to be unbridled and large, it wants
to leave behind the fears that occupy it,
all those stories, dark and bright,
in which its worth and weight
is questioned. only when it dreams
does it soar, supple and light,
by its very nature nearly song.

**translation**

is there a zone of darkness between all languages,
a black river that swallows words
and stories and transforms them?
here sentences must disrobe,
begin to roam, learn to swim,
not lose the memory that nests in
their bodies, a secret nucleus.
will the columbine's blue be a shade of violet
when it reaches the other side,
and the red bee balm become a pear, cinnamon-
sweet? will my tench be missing a fin
in the light of this new language? will it have to learn
to crawl or to walk upright?
does language know how to draw another toward it
or only how to turn the other one away? can each word,
then, risk the transit, believe itself
invulnerable, dipped in pitch and hard as steel?

## ljubljanica river of memory

leaning over the sluggish river,
familiar with the legends
of the triad of mountains, bridges
and linden trees, practiced in
fathoming that tender lament,
eyes fixed on the riverbed, are you searching
for your slovenian face,
for the one true story.
meanwhile, the water sinks
underground, changes names,
directions, shores, heavily burdened
with lances, clasps and axes.
the nightmare of earlier massacres
clings fatally to the river's trench. shattered
and bereft of custom,
vows and pleas drift downstream.
searching for yourself, you catch sight of
the other, warped and blurred,
flowing upward.

**barje moors**

one day the wind dropped,
the bluff did not move, heavy
rain came in from the south, an adder
crowned with flames scaled the mountain.
then a dugout canoe broke through
the cell wall of time, impaled it, and
disappeared. today, the scar that remained
is barely visible. salvaged from the mud,
a raft that traveled thousands of years
until it drifted before our eyes.
only now does a hawk swoop into the marsh.

## my grandfather's escape from the black sea

when you fell and sank ever deeper, into
the darkest waters, into the salt-heavy darkness,
did a current grab you or did you follow
your thoughts as they fled homeward
toward the alps? while you foundered, an end was declared
to the war that was never yours on the northern
shore of the sea that engulfed you. did you ever
arrive? ever reach the tide that, from the very beginning,
swept all losing armies through the gorge of the bosporus,
under the whorls of the dardanelles? did you follow
that spawn run north to the subterranean
rivers that sank like you? did you change
course or go ashore, not crossing the threshold
of your own home, this time as a trace of your old self
or a shy creature? where did you go on land,
which border turned you away or was it
the dead under its command, laid out in earthen barks
and set adrift, now awaiting the distant transit?
did you ever arrive? my mother believes
a strange man was gasping near the well at the poset farm.
she did not see him, but he was near.

**transit**

on the shores of the new land you will
discard your mother tongue. clouds that drift by
above will be echoes of words
you once spoke, but now
withhold. long after you are gone
the knights of the air will fulfill
the figments of your imagination,
love, worry, harmony,
as strange as the giants of la mancha. the house
you once lived in is a roughly
timbered frame of smoke. it hovers
over you, barely perceptible, imponderable, like you.
washed up on the shore, an old comb,
the wrong sock in the right shoe.
the crumpled horizon in your hand,
an island of garish paper.

*all is fulfilled with the word in which*
i expand, branch out. all
that has not been said, abandons me,
what has not been made clear
through language passes away.
a conglomeration of effort
suspended in an inference. unasked,
i take each word-step unevenly,
worming my way through my time, which
carries me off and disgorges me. the
presentiment of all calamity trapped
in a single cell. writing pushes its way
into the present, into the glare. when it falters
it reveals its old carapace of fear.

## ocean and poem

this poem will never grasp
the ocean nor its gushing spray
that scatters in pigments. it will
always be tiny. its verses will
resemble children's drawings, the horizon
a loose seam behind which the water
breaks into the abyss. laid hesitantly
and with an awkward line,
the sky light blue or gray.
the sun an orange bubble aswim in seething
air. the poem will hold on
to me and get its feet wet.
it will play with the crabs, find refuge
behind a shack of language,
from there we will watch the raging
waves and see the fear
in the eyes of the fishermen from balapitiya
fear that will follow us deep into the nights. suddenly
the poem will see more clearly, will
recognize the terrifying dreams I
brought back from the beach, in which
i dug up corpses that refused
to be washed away. it will lay its word-hand on

my shoulder and comfort me.
i will fall asleep in its arms and
withstand the howling dark.

**life-eater**

this poem is a life-eater,
it has devoured my years, all of them
vanished without a trace in its boundless
maw, it has sealed up my language,
knows more than i, has
fathomed more than i, has always
absorbed all that ever intruded into
its body—the rooster,
the snake, the egg, the hind,
the peacock, the hare, the dove.
this poem is no noah's ark
that will spit back out all it
holds. it is a hungry whale
that ploughs through languages
hunting for the word-light, the glinting verse.

**poem and sense**

this poem is numb, insensate,
it feels nothing as long as i do not exchange
its body for mine. only then
can it sense itself as a lump
in my throat, can its guise observe
through my eyes, how dully
the pictures I present to it shine, how
the spoken busies itself with the seen,
licks and woos it, how far ahead the doubts
i wanted to spare it have charged. we
aren't much without each other,
barely worth mentioning. where we should
be discernable, undetected emptiness reigns.

**mute poem**

has the voiceless poem slipped out of language
when it cradles me in its silence? lost in thought,
it wanders through my home, sets its composure
aside, hangs my glances like lanterns
in the autumn garden, adds up expired
seconds into eternities in which we
elude each other. as soon as i produce a
handsome phrase about the self or the
state of the world, language cuts
me short, forbids me any compliant
word that has not crossed the silence.
such poems are abashed, at a loss for words,
aimed simply at themselves and at me.

**house of love**

## night woman

i lie on the kitchen table
and hear noise. a door is opened
and light falls into the room.
pillows and boots are piled
a yard high on an unheated stove. now
i want to see where you let her sleep,
your wife calls out. you come in first,
your smile brushes
over the walls and me.
i seek refuge outside in the garden,
and hear someone screaming,
she loves you, she just doesn't know it!
it is raining on one side of the house.

**madrid disparates**

in the parque del retiro,
squirrels leap
from swinging branches.
we stand in the sparse
shadow of the pines,
beneath me a dancing horse
on the wire that holds it.

traffic surges
over the plaza de colón,
the dusty air fills
our lungs, weighs
down our steps with
lead. brown and beige
are this city's colors.

you won't like
the apartment, carmen says,
the splintering streetlamps
when the storm grabs them.
naked and clothed i lie
next to you. how false
appears all that was.

at dawn you embrace me
on the paseo del prado.
silly girl, let's
be reasonable, you say.
we will start at the end,
after our sinister dreams,
and will go from there.

## house of love

the house that shelters me breathes imperceptibly.
has a timbered roof that billows like a sail,
has an outer layer that is not rigid. you hear
me living inside it, you ask what i'm doing,
grumble when i remain silent and weep. in the house
of love, everyone builds their own little cottage,
one for themselves and another for a third.
i will no longer give in to persuasion. my ribs
have congealed into a fan vault
that barricades me in. you can hardly
detect me, i'm so distant from you.
at night, my old desire makes a racket
deep in the keel. i float inwards, where love
couples with the foreign, to the cape
of hope, my throat taught.

## appassionata

when your voice reaches my ear,
my lethargic heart startles
awake. my ears' limbs pulls you to me,
to catch in the depths of your breath
the familiar tremor that is now fading
and was at the beginning our prelude.
in a flash, my words fly up, swollen into an
orchestra. every sentence a
promise, an appassionata, wanting to be more
than merely said. enter my ear,
here you will be welcomed magna voce,
seen with all senses! even your
farewell is a bright chord, a
tender coda with a ritardando ring.

## house of desires

the house we dream of is far away.
it's small but with an echo chamber
where our voices swing on
musical scales, like forgotten verses
of love songs that have lost their
luster. every false note upsets
our feverish equilibrium. we listen
with vulnerable hearing
to the dust-rustle that washes
over the floor in waves and we hear
the emptiness intone a notturno.
the naked flapping of a butterfly wing
here where we are without one another
could build to a tornado.
we invent flowers and offer them to each other,
waterlilies that bloom on dry land,
cattails that swim in streams,
magnolias that take root on windowsills,
and we write each other cards from places
we happen to be, which we observe
for one another but still only half see.
our bouts of homesickness become ever milder
and in the process what unites us grows
as does what divides us.

**house of children at play**

at first you won't see the children
behind the shady wall.
we'll paint astonishing mythical creatures
on the capitals for you, winged horses
and fire-spitting dragons. rampant
ferns will lurk above you.
swarms of birds, like fish, will
dance through the elements in the updraft,
as you pass through the
rounded arches. we will line up all toys
before our door and sing a song
of deepest welcome.
come into the house of children at play,
i've been waiting for you such a long time!
with the passing of time, the rough-hewn
sandstone has taken on the colors of my fears,
light yellow and ocher and
red. the children have grown quiet,
as if dead. i circle in my previous
form, small, tough, with plump
legs and a quizzical mind.
as soon as you appear, the children
will step out of the twilight and call
our names: youandme youwithoutme mewithoutyou.

## love and grass

as if unintentionally, the finger-grass brushes
my upper arm with its fan-like hand.
shocked, i let the downy hair on my skin
defend itself and i stretch out next to it
in the grass. it trails its seed panicles
the length of my neck and deftly fans
the scent of grass towards me. thrusting
into my underarm it sinks its little teeth
into my warm skin. no herb has grown against
this passion. lying in this acidic soil
groaning, our husks burst and release
their fruit. the long lashes rise in the wind.
eyeless, it looks at me sadly,
it must be blinded by love!

**summer skirmish**

i have barely put my arm around you
on this lovely placid morning
when the fleet of bees begins its maneuvers.
behind our backs, a base camp tirelessly
spits out warriors. in the sky
motors howl, in a dogfight,
in a nuptial flight. wings are oiled,
glands overflow with missiles.
grenades of nectar fall on us
like sticky dew. before we take cover
a clownish squadron of bumblebees dawdles
behind the aircraft, their motors
sputtering, their probosces trumpet the retreat.
painted ladies bustle past in the lull of the battle
with milky wings, the black-veined whites
drop from every cloud, mince over the site of the slaughter
with a shudder and fly away.

## happy in sveti ivan

as long as I remain stretched out
in the shadow of the apse,
a ribbon of meadow ants will flow
through my veins. arterial walls
will echo with their most delicate steps.
bee beetles will take off their shaggy
furs and nest in the hair on my nape.
an ortolan will land on my forehead
and peck the biscuit crumbs from my lips.
or i could rise and stroke your
flanks, pull you to the dry fountain,
to the playgrounds where counting rhymes
can be heard and the sweet hum
of small children's voices. i could also
drop off to sleep and fall upward to the olive tree
leaves, small wings could sprout
in my armpits, which you will glimpse
when i wave to you mid-flight.

**rubbish and poppy**

how ordinary we have become.
every day we follow orderly courses
through the house, sweep breadcrumbs
from the table, hold wineglasses up to
the light and wipe down the sinks.
we pull hair from the drain, stack
bills on the shelves, trade
barbs and compliments.
although sometimes we speak
through the flower. our well-versed
legs press against each other, a
dark sap flows in our veins,
leaving red spots on our skin.
we hatch black seeds, childless
as we are. spores of drunkenness
swim in treacly spit,
that we spread over our bodies,
placing a purplish trace in hidden
nests, and as offspring our sighs.

**festival**

the noonday sun has drawn
a rainbow in my eye. in the hazy
light, all gestures made at the table
appear wrapped in pink tissue paper.
flies land on their backs
and rhythmically wave their
little legs. knowing they are
watched, they offer encores
by spinning like tops and waggle dancing.
behind us summer's backdrop
is raised. we fasten it
to the trees' spore-drunk crowns
and to the thorny old red moss.
i lean on my sentences,
keep an eye out for listeners.
sparks will be sent spinning
from our glasses into the temperamental sky,
which stalls in obscurity longer than expected.
a flash finally introduces the thunder.
the stage set drips after the magnificent
performance. an old scent of roses swims
in the shimmering puddles. we stand
under the firmament's torn base
with wet hair and cheer
the finale, which has fallen into the water.

## in the tower

i adorn the tower room
we live in with select words.
the table is cleared
and father's armor packed away.
his old army is camped far below.
at night, when i'm plagued by dreams,
i go into the dungeon.
i've imprisoned lovers there
in cages light and spacious.
i show up naked,
go from one bed to the next with the blank face
and silken cloth i was given as a gift,
have glistening traces of albumen
on my inner thigh,
smell of carnations and rotting apples,
hoping that someone will ask me
to wash before his eyes,
i wet my underarms, my pubic hair,
run a comb through my lurking eye-thickets.
stairs lead to me, which i push away
sentence by sentence. i hear the word-truss collapse,
hear its echo: i am yours, i am yours.
back in my bed

i forget the men's staring.
in these sheets that smell of us
every touch of your hands
rubs out my desolate memory.
you put away armored horses and wooden lions
in the closets, fill them with
hemlock, sage, chamomile.
with date biscuits, you keep me from
looking out the window
through which the seductive call sounds.

the invisible girl

i

first, take the wooden flooring on which you place
her, the hair clasps and hoops, the flyweight
of a tulle dress she likes to wear. take the first
page intricately filled with spidery script.
take the broken snail shell,
the horn of a ram, the silver button,
take the malt candies out of their box, her
gashed knee, throw it all together carelessly,
pile it up. just forget the name, it is not hers.

**ii**

when will they recognize your face, my
girl? you could still be an aquatic plant
in the developmental stage, with small growths
on your fingertips, which have only just learned to feel.
you breathe and speak, but your lips seem
to have fallen away. they remained unkissed
and overlooked on the day that woke you.
you invited the neighbor boy
to dance, he chose the other. had he taken you
in his arms, a tree bursting with blossoms day and night
would have sprung from your lips. if you were a miracle tree, my girl,
you'd have discarded yourself as a wish. onto the grass
out into the field with you, girl, oh my girl!

**iii**

you play the game of being missed,
crouching in a dark closet all day long,
so they'll look for you, you want, when
you're older, to not find your way home from a long
journey, so they'll say what an adorable girl she was,
the one who left the field of daffodils. you play
the game of disappearing, while wanting to be found.
your secret thoughts glow, your dream
has become a twin, who lives in your stead,
disregarded and sometimes even missed.

## iv

who am i, the girl asks the courteous
man looking at her intently. come,
the man says, i will make you
a body. and lays his hand on her delicate
shoulders, lays his hand on her meager breast,
pushes his finger into her hidden lap,
where the girl feels a movement
that continues in the emptiness. how can i ever
wipe away this hand, that makes me feel shame,
the girl thinks. will elderly hands
always intrude between me and my body?
how abandoned will it still be and
how long alone until it's mine again?

**v**

you are always ahead of me, mother,
i will never catch up with you,
patroness of my breath, sunflower,
pomegranate i broke open,
the girl prays. if you were to step
on me by mistake, i would fall like unripe fruit
from your tree of pain.
morning star, bird of paradise, rosebush
mine! you bud and help us day and night,
striking light, while i see
you as a towering mountain, a fire lily
revealing beauty. mother, what do you know of me,
i look into your burning glass,
show me your true face.

## leaving the isle of girlhood

the girl wants to climb the mountain, to go to gorice,
wants to be thrown into the sea, scattered
between the holm oaks and strawberry trees,
to be added as a shade of red to the colorless light,
which hovers untouched above the stone walls and
does not warm. her skull bones, split open,
want to release the memory
of her cool hands, of her
vow to never be anyone's wife.
her glowing hips also want to leave the cage
where they were confined until the day of unshackling.

i hear you coming as i release the girl.
you lift me onto your shoulder,
carry me to the festively lain table,
caress the child from my face,
feed me like a bride.

memory forget-me-not monument

## catchfly eyebright bird's eye

a grassy slope floods
my eyes with earth, pebbles
and grass, with flowers pink,
yellow-white and blue. i have forgotten
the names of all the plants
that flowed through me and could
not bear witness, nor testify
for them at some point. later,
much later, when the meadow floods
subside, words
like *lučca, smetlika, veronika*
can perch on the flowers
or appear unexpectedly
like thoughts that had veered
off course long before.
will i recognize them or spell
them back into silence?
will the meadow remember me,
will the flowers know my name?
i will fall into the chasm.
the meadow will replace me.

*on the shore path in the evening light—*
on which i stood one day,
at the end of a summer
that broke me open like a small
fruit (i was bitter and very tough)
– a mote of light falls on me
a spark from abiding time.

the impatiens still throws
its blossoms into the air like balls.
it tumbles down, sinks in the water
and disappears. a grain of light rises,
as it had back then and dies away.

the shore path is now built up, shifted,
torn out of the meadow and discarded.
i, too, have emerged repeatedly
as a translation of myself,
transferred and rewritten
i appear in a new transcription
although in a similar form.

the second of light takes flight,
the spark of a time that remains,
scatters and returns.

## when language left me

perhaps i was just drinking coffee
or opening the newspaper.
perhaps i was drawing the curtains
or looking out onto the street when it
left me. still i thought, what a rattling
from deep in the wall,
what a clattering in this room.
no windowpanes shattered,
no chairs toppled in the kitchen.
the names on street signs
vanished leaving only the ashes of letters.
a tanker filled with words retreated
above the houses, massive, silent,
my swollen tongue twitched
in my dry mouth.
i escaped from the city,
took refuge behind the border.
no letters arrived and no answers
were sent. a hole gaped
where i once was.
where i am now, my shadow
runs to seed.

**assumed name**

i learned street maps by heart
and winding paths. my skin
stretches white as if dyed with sand lime.
Horsetail buds break open between my nails
like signposts. words hum in the tent of skin
that covers me like a deceptive mask.
i beat the drums and shoot rocket flares
that blaze dangerously in my
eyes. a puff of air could rip this protective
screen from my body. it isn't fluttering yet,
others still believe they recognize me.
when my name is said, there will be
a white cloth in the landscape.
i was there.

**what was**

once a year,
when bookmarks
fall from my books
with notes like
fern-numbers,
carnation-registries,
nettle-clips,
i return to my village.

on opened pages
are yellowing stories
that have laid down their weapons,
the scorn, the uproar,
the dance-sweat
that drips from
the dancers' temples.

i put on my red smock,
pile my hair up
like a bush on the top of my head,
i wear dirty socks and
boots that could fit a man.
i smell the pork fat
in the unaired kitchens,
try out names
and their shadow-stories,
which, once they've begun,
clatter
like drifting wood.

i stopped at the entrance to the farm.
there i set down a stone
with a groove
filled with lime
to remind me
where I came from.

*it could be a woman who shows*
me the way to the village i seek.
it could be a village
with inns for strangers and
pairs of eyes to count.
it could be a village, one i know well.
yet my mother comes to me during the night.
she points toward the valley. all of this
does not belong to us, she says. my bags
are packed and stand by her door.
i recite verses about arriving.
they are neither songs nor complaints,
just vague sounds.

*nothing to be done, as always.*
while we grew, clustered
like columns rising towards
the heavy sky, which they wanted kept
at a distance, people close to us
fell. with bloodshot
eyes they sat and stared
at us, not knowing which
side of existence they were on.
we stuck gaudy post-its
on everything we saw, jotted down
sun, moon and earth, street, house,
forest or flower. what we discovered
stormed away, as if it had just been seen through.
years were torn from the calendar, rot
steamed from the sump, fumes that
always trailed us. while we grew,
the elderly endured the earth's invasion.

## memory, forget-me-not, monument

how much the torn-open field i
stand before betrays. the autumn sun
already pelts the clouds with resplendent
colors. even with eyes closed
its fiery complexion blazes. near
the farms i'm circling i look
for words discarded
like scrapped tools,
cull them, the way you gather
dried twigs from the forest edge and pile them
on the side of the road. mountain flanks grow
from the valleys to higher
peaks. in my voice
the first language crystalizes and
learns the codes of memory by heart:
*spomin, spominčica, spomenik.*
memory, forget-me-not, monument.

**talking with thistles**

my thistle-head hides
behind courteous sentences,
unrecognizable in its disguise,
unapproachable in its rebelliousness,
tedious in its reticence.
but appearances deceive.
i could tell you stories
from a thousand and one days,
audacious tales
that scramble over my churlish head
like frizzled thoughts
in a salto mortale. i
was tempted to talk myself into trouble
when you asked me
if i ever still thought of you.

but don't come too close!
my lines have hooks
that will crudely catch your ears
with spiky words and stalks,
my dear, when you beguile me
with loose lips.

## king matjaž visits his village

one day the old king left the mountain
to ensure that all was in order. he walked
through the village and greeted the residents,
now in this language, now in the other.
he saw little towers growing from the farmhouses,
now in this color, now in another.
seen from above, the little village looks
like a stone bouquet, the king said.
we also decorate our gardens with colorful
garlands, the mayor announced. our graves,
as you see, have become lawns for sunbathing. everything
turns to the good under the new king's reign. we celebrate
progress every month with fireworks.
the village band plays songs about the north pole and
the south pole, we also speak a common language
and have taken on new names. i, for example,
am now called nearby-recreation-area-maximizer. oh,
how nice, said the king, how marvelously
cheery! crossing the village square he lost his way
and stopped short in a moment of shock.
you're blocking the picture, a girl called
from the other direction, please step aside. i should
start to dance, the king thought, and raised his thin leg

several times. the king is dancing, the residents rejoiced,
he's finally begun to understand! lovely to be at home
again, the king waved goodbye
and laughed and wept and stepped into the shaft.

**village king**

the king slept in the cradle
that looked like a wood coffin.
he often complained as he lay down to sleep
that the bed was too small and undignified
and he'd be better off huddling under a tree
on the ground, in the dirt.
the following morning, he seemed to have forgotten it all,
drank strong coffee and smoked five cigarettes.
he assigned his courtiers tasks
with an air of apology.
you know, he said, it's not for me.
my wife will seize it all,
she doesn't sleep with me.
your highness should give her a beating,
his treasurer advised.
i should, yes, the king said,
and that evening he threatened before going to bed:
wife, i'll kill you if you don't show up,
i'll throw myself out the window,
and he fell out of bed.

## impresario

chestnut trees line the streets
he drove along before he entered his house
and played the parts in his head.
excited voices rose from the theater stalls
in his mind, where he trod
the stage. from the sounds he happily
followed the shifting fly systems, the audience's
breathing. i'm rehearsing, he would say, but never
that he was acting. he fought for every true
feeling before it ebbed away in the undertow of applause.
from every alley, the chestnut trees
gathered before his window when he
mapped out the great battles. one day in may
his life threw off its shadow, which he
smothered with spotlights.
no one stood between him and the world
he intended. the chestnut trees retreated into their
rows, the birds perched in them.
scattered clapping could still be heard,
the pattering of blossoms dropping
their petals. silence returned in a final
revenge, in triumph.

## king impersonator

the king reigns from the stage.
today he wants to present a piece
about the rise of his house.
he rehearses falling into the depths
from the ropes that hold him unseen.
in his mind's eye he sees the audience before him
and feels their stuffy breath.
he wants to fight for his opponent's applause
and hopes that his friends will forgive him.

the king rehearses for the showpiece
in which he won't die when he pretends to die.
gesturing extravagantly, he will fulminate against
lies and betrayal, he will solicit the love
he'd like to spurn with some mummery
that seeks his equals on the world's stages.
you'll see blood spurt
in a way you've never seen blood spurt before,
he will threaten.

we'll illuminate the horizon for him,
mark the center of the stage,
we'll applaud, distraught,
when he crashes to the ground
and thunder sounds at the right moment.
dying, he will tell of the agony it is to be king.
we will almost take fright
and raucously shout long live our king.

when the curtain falls,
he'll notice an abrasion
he has caused himself
in his attempt to persuade.
for a moment he will be at a loss.
no one knows how lonely i am,
he will say, no one feels what i feel.

**rageweed**

*(allegretto, con affetto)*

in the scraggiest field have i put down roots
and strangled the anger in my blossom-throat,
i've nodded and nodded,
was rattled by them all
rattleweed that i am,
shadow plant.
having choked down so much
i developed a goiter
in which the wind gets caught
and others' talk echoes.
my calyx has become a firecracker
that children explode between the palms of their hands
to everyone's amusement, to my outrage.
that's enough!
i'm going to seek out new fields
and evolve into a higher flowering in the new ground.
i don't want to become a low-lying daisy
or useless dog-fennel!
i want to fling my seeds
at everyone who passes
or spit poison and bile
at those who brush past.

impatient touch-me-not that I am,
a nettle without stinging hairs.
in my little heads and cups, i have explosive seeds
at the ready to sow weed epidemics
and rampant fields onto which i'll throw myself.
at night i will grow horns
instead of umbels. how beautiful, they'll say,
these horn tips are, red with rage, yellow with fury!
i'm already unfurling my pouch
and pushing my spit-seeds onto the tip of my tongue.
i discharge at once
i immediately shoot out from my fruit capsule!
i've become a measly weed,
base, disgraceful and very common.
that's what's ordinary about my nastiness.